HigherLife Publishing & Marketing focused on my best interest as one of their authors. Each person, at every level in the publishing process, is courteous and professional. You will never regret signing on with HigherLife.

—Dunbar

Auth... *...nsultant*

I attribute the success c...   ...gestions and professional guidance in which HigherLife marketed it. David Welday III and his staff will greet you at their office door or cheerfully answer any questions you may have on the telephone, both in a professional and family-like manner. I have once again placed my trust in David's staff for the publishing and distribution of my second book, *Looking Up to See the Bottom.*

—R. Dale Perkins
Author/Speaker

I have seen HigherLife bend over backward for their authors, even more than traditional publishers!

—Chris Robinette
Trade Sales Consultant

We have a very talented team at NTM and ANI, but we needed fresh ideas and innovation to move our products to a new level. From the first project, HigherLife gave us a new cover design and a marketing strategy that is beyond anything we have ever seen. HigherLife's editorial staff brought us a full-blown curriculum with so many incredible creative elements that the teachers will not want to teach anything else!

—Jody Crain
Non-profit Director

HigherLife Publishing offers a unique publishing menu that perfectly suited our needs. We have published two successful books, *The Teleios Man* and *The Table Experience*, with HigherLife Publishing. David Welday and his efficient team are committed to the best for their clients and deliver an excellent product. Their professionalism, quality publication, expertise, availability, advice and most of all warmth of relationships has made them the go-to place for us. We couldn't ask for a better publisher in which to entrust our message and ensure its success.

—Larry and Devi Titus
Authors/Speakers/Ministry Leaders

HigherLife was a joy to work with and I always felt I was in the hands of experts. They were very kind, patient, and thorough.

—Leon Franck
Author

The President of HigherLife is impressive. He is just what I needed. That includes the HL team, but starts with him.

—Thomas Wheeler
Author/Entrepreneur/Charitable Director

GET YOUR BOOK PUBLISHED!

GET _{YOUR}BOOK
PUBLISHED!

David W. Welday III

From Contracts to Covers, Editing to E-books, Marketing and Sales: What Every Writer and Author Should Know

HIGHERLIFE
DEVELOPMENT SERVICES, INC

Oviedo, Florida

Get Your Book Published! — From Contracts to Covers, Editing to E-books, Marketing and Sales: What Every Writer and Author Should Know
By David W. Welday III

Published by HigherLife Development Services, Inc.
400 Fontana Circle
Building 1, Suite 105
Oviedo, FL 32765
(407) 563-4806
www.ahigherlife.com

ISBN 13: 978-1-939183-00-2
ISBN 10: 1-939183-00-6
First Edition

10 11 12 13 — 9 8 7 6 5 4 3 2 1
Printed in the United States of America

Content categories:
Book Publishing
Book Marketing
Leadership
Platform
Public Speaking

TABLE OF CONTENTS

Introduction

Do you have a message burning inside of you? Do you have an area of expertise or inspiration you know would make a difference in people's lives, if you could just "get it out there"? That feeling, that motivation, is what most often inspires people to write a book. If you have something encouraging, exciting, compelling, maybe even life-changing that you want to share with more than just your immediate circle of friends, it's important that you do the very best job possible in getting it published and brought to market the right way. This book will help you.

I've been involved in publishing for longer than I care to confess. I've seen it done well and I've seen it done poorly. I've seen authors experience the joys of becoming a *New York Times* Bestselling Author, which can be a ton of fun! However, I've seen far more new authors end up frustrated that after all the hard work and pouring out of their soul, they have a garage full of books, less money in their bank account, and a heart full of dreams forced to sit on the shelf along with their unsold books.

My goal is to explain, in plain English, how book publishing works and to equip you with information you need to succeed. I hope to help you avoid some of the pitfalls that have waylaid so many authors along the way.

I also want to commend you for your courage in taking the first steps toward publishing your book. I wish you all the best and, if at any point along your journey, you have questions, please don't hesitate to let me know. I love to encourage others along their journey of becoming a successfully published author.

CHAPTER 1

Why Write a Book

Before you start typing, I believe it's important to step back and check your motivation for wanting to publish a book. If your primary motivation is to become famous and make a lot of money, you may want to reconsider your decision. Oh sure, there are many people in the world who have done just that—become a bestselling author and made a lot of money. But they are the exception, not the rule. Think of it this way. For all the thousands of wide-eyed and eager youth who play basketball and dream of playing in the NBA, only a microscopic percentage of them actually achieve that dream. Some achieve some success and make it as far as the NCAA, but the vast majority of "ballers" go no further than driveway and community center pick-up games. And yet, they can still have fun and success playing the game even without making it into the limelight of the NBA and the "big money". With this in mind, my advice to you is to pursue publishing for something other than the pursuit of fame and fortune.

I would submit that the top three reasons to pursue getting published are:

1. You simply enjoy the process of writing and communicating your thoughts with others in a way that brings value, benefit, and blessing to those who read what you have to say.

2. You have obtained a level of expertise in your field and you feel compelled to share that information with others. Again, there is that sense of wanting to make the world a better place or to bring benefit to other people's lives from what you have learned on your own.

3. You recognize that being a published author can offer a level of status and market exposure that can open doors of opportunity, can provide you a positional advantage with your competition, and positions you to be a "thought leader" in your field that can bring benefit, not just to your readers, but to you and/or your organization.

So, before you go any further, step back and get honest with yourself about your motivations behind writing a book. Write them down. Be clear about them. The more specific, the more clear you are in understanding why you're getting into publishing, the better choices you will make in how you publish your book and how you market your book throughout the process.

Don't Miss This...

Before you go any further, I suggest that you get out a notebook or open a Word document and create what I will refer to as your "publishing playbook". This is a summary document where you outline basic information about your book, your audience and your message.

Title the first section in your playbook, "Why am I Writing this Book?" Answer that question candidly and date it. Take time to give serious thought to this question. It will be important that you have this sense of direction, motivation or inspiration clearly resolved in your heart and mind.

This document, this publishing playbook, will become a helpful tool that you complete throughout the publishing process, so keep it with you as you move forward.

CHAPTER 2

Five Key Questions Every Author Must Answer

I've found that authors often dash down the road of writing and publishing a book without thinking through some very critical questions that, if artfully and articulately answered, will help them become much more successful. So, pull out your publishing playbook and answer these five key critical questions. I ask any author, who publishes with our company, to answer these specific questions. As a publisher, it's extremely helpful for me to know how an author answers these questions.

1. Who is your intended audience?
2. What is the central benefit to the reader?
3. What is the unique message of your book?
4. What is the burning passion behind your book?
5. What marketing opportunities do you have to sell the book?

1. Who Is Your Intended Audience?

Take a moment to think about the typical person to whom you are writing. What is their age, gender, ethnicity, social/economic status? What are the common areas of influence that bind them together? Are they all conservative, politically? Are they all of a certain spiritual persuasion? Do they all enjoy water sports or have a fondness for Thai food? Resist the temptation to think that your book will appeal to everybody. It won't. But, even if your message will indeed have a very broad appeal to a wide segment of the population, for this exercise, identify who you think will be the *most likely* reader of your book. Don't think about a generic, general audience of people. Think about a specific person. I know, I know. You're convinced that the whole world wants to read your book. And that may be true. But the more specific you can be in identifying your most likely reader, or what I would refer to as your "raving fan", the more successful you will be. So, in your publishing playbook, in not more than a paragraph or two, write down a description of your primary target audience.

It may be that you have a secondary audience that you think would be interested in your book. For example, maybe you are writing a book for owners of a dental practice to help them be more successful and understand best practices in running their dental office. Dentists who own their own practice may be your primary audience. But maybe the same information that you would share with dental practice owners would also be helpful information to owners of other types of small businesses such as a real estate broker, CPA or insurance broker. So, while you may have a primary audience that you intend to reach, there may be one or more secondary audiences your book will also benefit. But avoid the temptation to make your book so generic and appealing to everyone that you end up not truly capturing the attention of anyone.

2. What Is the Central Benefit to the Reader?

You know what your book is about. But the focus here is not on what's in your book or what your book is about, but *how your book will help the reader.* How will your message help make their life better? Will it make them smarter, sexier, thinner, happier, or richer? You need to be very clear about what your book promises to do for the reader. Maybe, if you've written a great American novel, the highest benefit is to thoroughly engage and entertain your reader for several hours, to give them a welcomed escape from the hustle and bustle of their daily reality. That's fine. But be clear and specific about that.

New authors must have a good handle on why a complete stranger, who has never met them, would be willing to plunk down $15–$25 of their hard earned money to pay for what they have to say. The stronger, the more clearly you can state what is your book's compelling benefit, the more you will attract readers to what you have to say.

Being able to clearly articulate the central benefit of your book will be essential to your marketing efforts, as well. You will need to fully grasp the central benefit of your book in order to write the back cover copy, run ads, write a press release, promote the book online, and engage people so they want to order your book. Consider making a list of all the benefits you think your book will offer to readers. Now rank those benefits in order of priority, with the most important benefit at the top of the list and the least important benefit at the bottom of your list. Show the list to others who have read your manuscript or heard you talk about the plan and plot of your book. Ask their opinion. Sometimes you may be too close to it and may not even be aware of the real take-away or benefit your book offers. Take time to work this through.

3. What Is the Unique Message of Your Book?

The message of your book ties in with the central benefit to the reader. In your publishing playbook, write down what you are going to say that hasn't been said a thousand times before—or how are you going to say it differently? How are you going to make your book compelling to read?

For example, if I ask you to think of a book about the differences between men and women and, trust me, there have been hundreds, maybe thousands of them written, I suspect that one book will most likely come to the top of your mind and that is John Gray's book, *Men are from Mars, Women are from Venus*. Why is that? Is it because John Gray had such revelatory information that no one had ever thought of before? No. It's not that he said things that nobody had ever said before. It's just that he found a unique and clever way to say it; a way that people connected with. How many feel good devotional books have you read or encountered in your life? And yet, *Chicken Soup for the Soul* has become a franchise brand that has made Jack Grandfield and Mark Victor Hansen rock stars in the area of book publishing. Was it just that they had keen insights to life that nobody had before? I suspect not. I think it has more to do with the fact that they had a unique way to say what they had to share.

Now, try to summarize, in one sentence, your target audience, central benefit and unique message of your book. Perhaps you've heard of the elevator speech? It's essential that an author can immediately recite their "elevator speech" on what their book is about. The elevator speech is that 1–2 sentence speech that exactly describes what your book is about, who it's for, and how exactly it will affect the reader. (If you got on an elevator and someone asked you what your book was about, could you give them the answer before you reach the 5th floor?) This isn't as easy as it sounds! But, take time right now and work on that elevator speech. After your book is published, you will be repeatedly asked, "So, what's your book about?" You need to be ready to give a compelling, concise answer that will tease the person in front of you to want to know more. Here's a simple formula: To (state your target audience), my book offers (state your central benefit), by sharing (state your unique message).

4. What Is the Burning Passion Behind Your Book?

I challenged you to identify your motivation for writing a book in chapter one. With that motivation in mind, ask yourself these questions:

- What's the burning passion behind writing this book?

- Why do I feel compelled to sit at my computer for hours at a time to write this book?

Sometimes, personal motivation becomes part of the story. If readers understand why you wrote the book, it will make them more interested in reading what you have to say. At HigherLife, we have a client who runs a funeral home and he wrote a book for families who had recently lost a loved one. He wrote the book to encourage them. Early on in his life, this client tragically lost his own brother to suicide. So, what was his motivation? In part, it was walking through his own personal tragedy and loss that led my friend to decide to write a book that would be helpful to others who went through the loss of a loved one. Knowing his personal story actually gives him credibility and makes me want to read his story even more.

Of all the things you could write about, of all the things you could share with complete strangers, why this topic? I think it's important that you have this settled in your mind and be able to articulate it in your publishing play book.

5. What Marketing Opportunities Do You Bring To the Table?

Nobody—not your publisher, not your publicist, not your best friend—nobody should be as passionate about seeing your message get into the hands of the people who need it most more than you. *You* must be your greatest cheerleader for your message.

I run into authors all the time who with genuine humility say, "It's not about me. I don't feel comfortable promoting my book. I'm not a promoter. I'm not comfortable talking about myself or my book." While I respect their intentions and sincerity, to them I say, "Then don't write a book." Because if you, as the author, are not convinced that your book is worth taking the time and money to read, and you are not willing to passionately say so, if you don't think your message has enough value to be worth taking the time and money to read, then why should anyone else? I'm not asking you to become a type-A personality promoter. That might not be who you are. But you need to decide right now and establish in your own heart and mind that you're going to do whatever it takes to get your message out to the marketplace to those who need it most.

If you get nothing else out of this book, understand this: As a general rule, *publishers do not market authors*! Even when and if you get a publishing deal, and your publisher is very excited about your message and seeing it developed and made available for sale with excellence, publishers largely do not invest their time and money in marketing authors. They would much rather invest in (translation, pay larger royalty advances) someone who already has a market or is willing to aggressively do their own marketing. So, decide right up front that you're going to do whatever it takes to get your message out into the marketplace.

acknowledgments literary editing manuscript promotion strategy acquisitions Board press run marketing advance run back-of-the-room sales bleed book block brick-and-mortar retailer advertising cover design develop

14

We'll spend a lot more time later in this book talking about creative ways that you can do that. But, my first encouragement to you is to start making a list of every contact you have that might possibly be interested in buying your book, endorsing your book, promoting your book, or telling others about your book in some way. Chances are, when you put your mind to it, you'll be amazed at how many contacts you have. Maybe your neighbor up the street is a successful insurance agent that has over 10,000 clients. Maybe your aunt is the head of a corporation that has 1,500 employees and 500,000 customers. Think about all of the connections you have and how many of those connections have access to large segments of your target audience. It will be especially important, when we talk about the marketing of your book, to know how to approach these people about your book.

In making your initial contact list, consider:

- Where did you go to school? It may benefit the alumni association to tell other alumni that you've become a published author.

- What associations do you belong to?

- What clubs are you a member of?

- How many clients have you helped and/or served?

- What church or charitable organizations are you a part of or affiliated with?

- More importantly, who are your friends that have access to the market?

CHAPTER 3

The Three Types of Publishing

The world of publishing has changed quite a bit in recent years. Many people feel the industry is in decline. I don't agree. I think there's never been a better time to publish—but how you publish is changing. You have more options. Technology, the economy, the internet and just how we live life have all collaborated to bring change to the industry and candidly, to open up new publishing options and opportunities to consider.

Publishing is not a one-size-fits-all proposition. You have options and should have a clear understanding of the various ways to pursue getting published.

Rather than making our discussion more complex than it needs to be, I'd like to simplify our discussion by lumping your publishing options into three main categories:

1. Traditional publishing
2. On-demand or self-publishing
3. Collaborative or partner publishing

1. Traditional Publishing

This is the form of publishing that most people are familiar with. To get published traditionally, you will most likely need to secure the services of a literary agent. Can you present your book proposal directly to a publisher without going through an agent? In some cases, yes. But most traditional publishers don't accept what the industry calls "unsolicited manuscripts". They don't have time to review hundreds, even thousands, of manuscripts, 99% of which won't be a good fit for them to publish. Traditional publishers have acquisition editors who are always out looking for potential projects to publish, but they don't typically like having an author come to them. They would rather work with a professional agent who essentially pre-screens proposals so that only solid proposals, that fit what the publisher is looking for, get through the front door for consideration.

What do I mean by traditional publisher? This is a publishing house where, if they accept your proposal, they will invest their money to see your message developed and brought to market. How good is that? Somebody literally invests their own money to develop your message into a polished work and bring it to market. But, there is a catch.

First, if a company is going to invest their money in publishing your message, they're going to require you to assign all of the publishing rights to them. And that's not an unfair thing to ask. I mean, if they're investing their money, then they want to have the final say how that message is presented. So, while your book may be copyrighted in your name, meaning you will own the intellectual property rights to your message, you will sign a contract with the traditional publisher that states that the publishing rights to your message in all forms and languages, both known and unknown, here and throughout the world, are transferred to the publisher. This means that they get to decide whether it's going to be hardback or paperback, how it's going to be edited, how it's going to be titled, what the cover's going to look like, if it's going to be sold as an e-book or not, where it will be sold, at what price, and where you will be allowed to sell the book and what price you will pay the publisher to buy any copies of your book to sell yourself. You no longer have the right to do anything you want with your message because you have assigned those rights exclusively to your publisher. So, be aware that to get a traditional publishing deal you are going to have to trade away, or assign, your publishing rights to that publisher.

You also need to know that the publishing world largely depends upon the mainstream book store sales channels to see your book distributed. Those book stores work on a long lead time and so, from the time that you receive a book publishing contract, it will most likely going be somewhere between 15–24 months before your book actually ever finds its way onto a bookstore shelf. It doesn't have to take that long but, with traditional publishers, it typically does. So, if you have a conference you're speaking at or there is a market driven need to have your book out within 6–8 months, working with a traditional publisher isn't likely to be a viable option for you.

The biggest challenge to getting a traditional publishing deal is that less than 1% of all authors can actually get a traditional publishing contract. Maybe you've written a brilliant novel or a phenomenal book on how to have a successful marriage or how to make the most amazing recipes ever savored. But if you're not well known, the chances of you getting a traditional publishing deal are extremely slim. You will be largely ignored. Brad Pitt or Angelina Jolie (or any highly visible, famous or well-known person), could write the same book, which might not be nearly as good as what you have written, and traditional publishers will be clamoring all over themselves to get a publishing deal for them. Why? **Because publishers aren't buying your message as much as they are buying your access to the market!**

You see, publishers don't want to invest potentially $40,000–50,000 of their money to develop your message and then have to invest even more money to gain media awareness and exposure for someone who doesn't already have any kind of existing market presence or audience. They would much rather pay a higher royalty to somebody who already has a media platform they know they can count on to bring exposure for the book. The publisher knows they can spruce up the manuscript/message to make it successful. So in a sense, the traditional publisher is buying access to the author's audience as much as, or more than, they are buying access to their message.

You may be surprised to learn that even with all their experience and expertise, publishers are more often wrong than right when it comes to picking what sells. For example, if a typical traditional publisher puts out 100 books a year, the top 10–15% of their lineup sells really well. Maybe it sells 100,000 copies, maybe a million copies. Everybody is making money and everybody is happy. Maybe another 25% of their lineup sells OK; at least enough for the publisher to recoup their initial investment, but nobody is taking trips to Tahiti. But the bottom 50–65% of the publishers' lineup didn't work out for them. In other words, they invested a lot of time and money to develop a message, had their sales teams present the upcoming new title to the book buyers of major bookselling outlets to get copies placed on store shelves. But people didn't come in off the streets looking for that book and so, after 60–90 days of sitting on a store shelf, the bookstores simply returned the books for full credit. Now the publisher is left holding excess inventory that they can't easily sell. So what do they do? They probably remainder their excess inventory, meaning they sell it for a few cents on the dollar, write off their losses and move onto the next title.

Most traditional publishing houses lose money on a high percentage of their lineup. The good news for them is that they make enough money on the top 10–15% of books published that it all comes out in the wash.

Even if you are fortunate enough to be in that very small percentage of authors who can actually secure a traditional publishing contract, there is still a high likelihood that your book won't sell well, you'll land in the bottom 50–65% of their author pool and be frustrated that you can't find your book on any store shelves and aren't getting any significant book sales (which translates into royalty checks), and since you assigned your publishing rights to the publisher, you are still buying your own book back from them at whatever author buyback price they set and you can't just do whatever you want with your own message. You're probably calling the publisher and asking why they don't spend more money marketing your book. But they won't. They've moved on to trying to find another book they think will sell better than yours did. In other words, you're stuck.

2. On-demand or Self-publishing

While only a microscopic percentage of would-be authors can get a traditional publishing contract, on the other end of the spectrum, we have on demand/digital or self-publishing where virtually anyone can get published. Digital printing technology today has given rise to a whole new genre of publishing, sometimes referred to as "on-demand" publishing. The phrase "on-demand" refers to the fact that instead of printing large quantities of books and storing them, books can be digitally printed only after an order for a book is placed. This allows publishers to not have to tie up their capital in printing and storing books that may never sell. Digital printing is easier than ever. Anyone can take a manuscript, typeset it, put a cover on it, and get a very small number of copies printed digitally. In fact, there are hundreds of companies out there who will be happy to charge you a fairly nominal publishing fee and for that fee, they'll make you a published author. But as with traditional publishing, there's a catch…

Most authors are not aware of the tremendous amount of thought, strategy, time, and effort it takes for even a good message to be properly massaged, edited, designed, positioned and marketed in such a way that it can be a successful selling book. In other words, what you don't know as an inexperienced author can get you into a lot of trouble. If you go to a self-publishing or on-demand publisher that takes your book, gets it typeset, designs a cover, and gets you anywhere from 10–100 copies back, once you get past the initial thrill of seeing your name on the cover of a book, what you may find you're left with is a book that wasn't as artfully developed or crafted as it needed to be. And you don't usually have a strategy for selling it. You counted on your publisher selling thousands of copies for you. But that rarely happens. The self-publisher takes your money, gives you a few books, possibly makes the book available for bookstores to order if someone requests a copy and moves on to the next paying customer.

Most self-publishers only make enough money to survive by signing up thousands of eager first-time authors who pay them a modest amount of money to get their book developed. The publisher moves on because they're not invested in an ongoing relationship with you or in taking the time to provide all the crafting and marketing that your book needs to succeed. If they did, you would be paying a lot more than what the on-demand/digital publisher is charging you. Self-publishers like I am describing here cannot afford to invest in helping you properly craft, copy edit, proof edit, design, position, and market your book with the minimal fees they charge. The old adage is true: you get what you pay for.

On the upside, with most self-publishers, you do get to keep most, if not all, of the publishing rights to your message. This is a benefit because you can choose to do whatever you want with that message. On the downside, your publisher isn't helping you make the best development, creative and strategic marketing decisions for that book, at least not in the same way you would expect with a traditional publisher. Self-publishing is typically the best option for the person who doesn't anticipate selling a lot of books. They want to get their book done with a minimal investment and plan on selling the book themselves. Because the author retains the publishing rights, he or she always has the option to pursue other publishing options down the road without being obligated to the self-publisher.

3. Collaborative or Partner Publishing

There is a third option that is surfacing for new authors that is sometimes called collaborative or partner publishing. This publishing option is more similar to traditional publishing, but with some of the benefits of self-publishing. Collaborative publishing attempts to bring you the best of both traditional and self-publishing, while minimizing the respective downsides of those two publishing options. With partnership publishing, you typically sign with a publisher who works closely with you to properly craft and develop your message in a similar process and excellence of quality that you would expect from a traditional publisher. In most collaborative publishing contracts, however, you are allowed to retain the publishing rights and also get your book published in a shorter time frame than you would expect with a self-publisher.

Collaborative publishers don't typically charge you a publishing or development fee as self-publishers do, but they do require that you purchase some quantity of books for your own sales and distribution purposes, usually, a few thousand copies or more.

Collaborative publishers typically invest much more time with your message than a self-publisher, working closely with you to make it shine. This can include ghostwriting, rewrite editing, content editing, proof editing, whatever is needed. You'll have much more flexibility and creative options in how the book is designed as well. Equally important, collaborative publishers can do more to help you market your book, sometimes even more than what traditional publishers offer. They have a similar ability to traditional publishers in getting your book presented and sold to bookstores and distributors. (We'll talk more about sales channel in a later chapter). A collaborative publisher also allows you to retain your publishing rights because, after all, it's not only your message, but it is also your marketing that's going to make the book successful. The ideal collaborative publisher will come alongside you to help you develop your book to its highest potential throughout the entire publishing process.

In collaborative publishing, as with self-publishing, you are able to get your book from concept to print in a much shorter time frame, typically four to eight months. Again, this is much faster than what you expect with traditional publishing.

Since with collaborative publishing the author is typically required to purchase at least a few thousand copies of their book from the initial press run, this method works best for an author who feels confident that they can sell at least 1,000–1,500 books through their own efforts. Once you've sold that many copies of your book, you've probably sold enough to recuperate 100% of what you invested in your initial press run. For example, if you buy 3,000 books that retail for $15 each and those books cost you $5 a piece, once you've sold 1,000 copies, you've paid for your entire press run and stand to make $30,000 in profit selling the remaining 2,000 copies. Not a bad deal!

I've worked with authors who initially published traditionally and then switched to collaborative publishing for their next book. I've also worked with self-published authors who went the collaborative route on subsequent books. It just depends on the specifics of your circumstances to determine what the optimal publishing route is for you.

For the author who sells a lot of books through their own efforts, collaborative publishing is usually the best option, even if they can attract the interest of a traditional publisher. Here's why: in traditional publishing agreements, you are typically locked into a fixed percentage discount that you can purchase books from your publisher. Perhaps you have a $15.95 book and your contract allows you to order 100 or more copies at a 60% discount. That means you will always be purchasing copies of your book to sell through your own efforts for $6.38 per book. But with a collaborative publisher, you may pay $4–$7 on your initial press run, but after that, your cost per book can drop to $2–$4 per book! So in the long run, you wind up making more money on your author sales of your book with a collaborative publisher than with a traditional publisher. If your traditional publisher is selling hundreds of thousands of copies for you through the bookstore, you probably don't mind paying a bit more on the copies you sell. But if you find yourself being the primary seller of your book, then it can be frustrating to have to purchase books from your publisher at a higher rate than you have to.

Again, each type of publishing—traditional, collaborative, and self-publishing, all offer unique advantages and challenges, so it's important to think through what is the best publishing partner for you. If you have any questions about any aspect of publishing, don't hesitate to call our office. We have publishing consultants who'd be more than happy to help you find the best way to go—and there's never a charge for the initial consultation!

CHAPTER 4

Publishing Contract

Once you have a publisher or perhaps a few publishers that you are considering signing with, you will need to negotiate your contract with them. So let's take some time to talk through the basic elements of any publishing agreement. Keep in mind that each contract will be slightly different for each publisher. You have the right to ask for revisions to be made to the agreement to meet your needs. The publisher can give on some terms and on some terms they likely won't budge. If you are working with a literary agent, it will be their responsibility to handle the contract negotiations for you, representing your best interests. You, however, should have a basic understanding of the major components of any publishing agreement. Let's take a look at what you need to know.

First of all, understand that a contract is negotiable. You do not have to sign on the dotted line or be in fear that the publisher will drop your book if you ask questions or push back with a change you'd like to make on the contract. First time authors tend to feel a bit intimidated by a contract, especially a lengthy one. If you have a simple question about your contract, feel free to call us. We're always happy to help you understand publishing contract language.

Some publishing contracts can be quite extensive, 15–20 pages long. Others are fairly simple. Typically, traditional publishers have longer contracts to cover their rights and options more thoroughly. This is to be expected because a traditional publisher is investing 100% of their money in getting your message developed and distributed, so they want to have more protection of their rights. Truth be told, every time a publisher gets burned, they change their contracts to cover whatever loophole or situation caused them to run into trouble and that's why traditional publishers have developed rather lengthy contracts that cover almost any eventuality or hazard you can think of (or might never have thought of!) Whether your contract is two or twenty pages long, there are a few basic components of the contract you should be aware of and that will matter most to you.

Let's look at the essential publishing contract in five categories:

1. Rights
2. Royalties
3. Advance
4. Buybacks
5. Options

1. Rights

The rights clause of a contract outlines who has control over and final say so over certain aspects of the book. For example, with a traditional publisher, you will essentially be assigning all of your publishing rights to the publisher. What this means is that, while the book may be copyrighted in your name so that you're the holder of the intellectual property, you have granted to the publisher the rights or determination of what can be done with that intellectual property. For example, the publisher will likely have the right to determine how the book is edited, how the book is titled, how the book is packaged, and what the book will sell for, including copies that you want to sell. In other words, when you want to sell your books at a speaking engagement, you will have to buy your own book back from the publisher, typically at a percentage off normal pricing. The rights clause also determines that only the publisher can do anything with the message. So, for example, if you want to take your message and turn it into a personal devotional or a work book or use it in some other fashion, you can't do that without the publisher's permission, if you have transferred all of the publishing rights of that message to the publisher. So the rights clause is very important and you want to be very clear in what you are signing away when you give rights to your publisher. The rights clause will specify who has the right to develop new products that are based on the message of your book. These are sometimes referred to as ancillary rights.

I want to take this thought a little deeper for the sake of explanation. Let's say a Hollywood movie producer comes to you and decides they want to do a major motion picture based upon your book. Pretty exciting, huh? Only problem is, if you gave the rights to that message over to the publisher, you don't have the rights to negotiate a deal with the Hollywood producer because the motion picture rights were likely assigned to your publisher.

If you ask your publisher before you sign the contract for video and movie rights, a publisher may be willing to negotiate with you and allow you to keep certain specified rights. But, unless you negotiate to keep specified publishing rights, don't assume that they are yours. Publishing contracts typically have all rights to your message transferred to the publisher.

You will want to clarify with the publisher under what circumstances you can get your rights back. For example, if the book is no longer readily available for sale or in print, do the rights automatically revert back to you or if you request the rights back, are they given to you for free or do you have to pay to get them back? These are things you should be aware of and be prepared to negotiate with your publisher.

Typically, with on demand/self-publishers, one of their selling points is that they allow you to keep all of your publishing rights. With collaborative publishers, some of them allow all the rights to remain with you and others require that the rights be assigned to the publisher or some combination of shared rights. Just make sure you pay attention to the rights clause of any publishing contract and make sure you're comfortable with those terms before signing anything.

2. Royalties

Royalties are the amount of money you receive for every book the publisher sells. Royalties are typically a percent of either the retail price or the net sales of the book. Here's the difference. Royalties based on retail are typically a lower percent, but based on a higher dollar volume, whereas, royalties based on net sales means the royalty is not paid on the retail value of the book, but on what the publisher actually collects from its sale of the book after accounting for all discounts. For example, note the following chart:

RETAIL PRICED BASED ROYALTY
$14.95 book x 10% royalty = $1.49 to the author
NET SALES BASED ROYALTY
$14.95 book x 50% book store discount = $7.47 x 10% = $0.75

In my experience, general market publishers typically pay royalties off of the retail price of the book and publishers working in the religious/Christian arena usually pay royalties off of the net sales price. One is not better than the other. You just have to pay attention to the number on which royalties are based.

One thing to look for in any royalty clause is what are called escalators. Escalators are the points at which sales of the book are strong enough that the royalty rate increases. For example, a royalty contract that pays you 15%, 18%, and 20% royalties in 25,000 increments means that you will get 15% royalties on the first 25,000 copies sold, 18% royalties on the next 25,000 copies sold, and 20% royalties on all copies sold by the publisher beyond 50,000 copies. Since the publisher has a significant amount of development costs in getting your book published, they will count on selling at least 10,000–20,000 copies in order to recoup the money they invested in getting your book developed, so the royalty rates are going to be lower initially so that the publisher can more quickly recoup their development costs. But once those costs have been recouped, the publisher is actually making more money on every book sold. If your book takes off in strong sales above the 20,000–50,000 mark, a publisher is often willing to share a higher percentage of the profit with you. Of course, they also want to give their authors the incentive to work tirelessly to help promote sales of the book, knowing that giving you a higher royalty when the sales volume reaches a certain level will encourage you to get out there and "press the flesh" and promote your book.

3. Author Advance

The principle of paying advances on royalties started when authors needed time away from their jobs or other projects to do the necessary research and background development in writing a book. Publishers would advance to the author some amount of money they expected to pay out in royalties after the book was published in order for the author to be able to devote time to getting the book written. This is still true, particularly with best-selling novel writers. Nowadays, authors come to publishers with manuscripts already written, but they still have hopes and expectations that they'll receive an advance on their royalties.

The market is changing and publishers are not nearly as liberal as they once were in handing out hefty royalty advances. Chances are, unless you are a very well-known personality or have a strong, proven track record in selling a ton of books, you're not likely to get any kind of advance on your royalties. If you do, great! The publishers are already risking their dollars to develop your book and, to advance you money in the hope that your book sells, only adds to their financial risk. Think of the royalty advance as nothing more than a loan. It's the publisher paying you up front for royalties they're counting on having to pay you a year or so down the road as your books sells. So, given the choice between a higher royalty and a higher royalty advance, it would make sense to opt for the higher royalty rate because, in the long term, that means more money in your pocket.

One of the main reasons that authors and agents tend to push for higher royalty advances (besides the fact that the agent gets paid their fees as a percentage of the royalties and advances they negotiate for the author), is that the higher the advance the publisher gives, the more likely they're going to work hard initially to promote, distribute, and sell the book. Your publisher will want to recoup their royalty advance as quickly as possible. Usually a higher advance is an indicator of the publisher's confidence that they are prepared to aggressively work to promote the book so that they can recoup their royalty advance paid out. Royalty advances aren't likely to be much more than 80% of what the publisher anticipates paying out in first year royalties. Perhaps it will help to look at some numbers:

Projected number of books sold in first year	10,000
Retail sales price	$14.95
Projected first year retail sales	$149,500.00
Royalty percentage	10%
Projected first year royalties	$14,950.00
Advance offered based on 80% of projected first year royalties	$11,960.00

Given this formula, if your publisher offers you an advance higher than $12,000, you can be fairly confident they're anticipating sales higher than 10,000 units in the first year.

Typically, only traditional publishers pay royalty advances. On-demand/self-publishers, and collaborative publishers may pay royalties on the books they sell for you, but they don't typically offer royalty advances.

Remember, royalties are paid to you only on the copies that the *publisher* sells. Royalties are not paid on copies that you sell. In addition, any copies that are used for promotional purposes or are sold at extremely deep discounts (typically greater than 60%), may get little or no royalties paid out on those sales. Royalties are not paid on returns either. So, if 10,000 copies are sold into the stores, but the stores later return 4,000 of those copies, then your royalties will be paid on the net sales of the 6,000 copies that were sold and not returned.

4. Buybacks

The buyback rate is the discount the publisher gives you when purchasing your book to sell through your own efforts. That's right; regardless which publishing venue you choose, you will have to pay for books that you want to personally sell.

We'll talk more about the ways you can generate author sales in a later chapter, but as the author of the book, you should plan on selling your book directly in as many places as possible. It's better for you financially. Think about it. If the publisher sells your books for you, and you receive a royalty percent (typically 10%–25% of either the retail price of the book or the net amount received by the publisher), you might make between $.50 and $2.00 per book. However, if you sell the book yourself, you keep 100% of the money received!

For example, if you are selling your book for $15 and paying your publisher $7.00 per book, then you will make a profit of $8.00 per book instead of the royalty of $.50 to $2.00 per book. In short, you make much more money selling your book directly than counting on your publisher to sell the book for you.

For a ballpark estimate on buybacks, an author buy-back discount typically starts at 50% and can go as high as 80–90% with most buybacks being in the 60–70% range. Obviously, the more you commit to buying, the deeper the discounts you can expect to receive on the books that you buy from your publisher. This makes sense because, the more books that you purchase, the less risk the publisher is taking on.

It's very important, in your author buyback clause, to be clear on where you, as the author, can sell your books and where you authorize the publisher to sell your books. Most publishers don't want to find themselves competing with their own author for sales and so it's important to spell out very clearly where you can sell the book versus where the publisher can sell the book and be sure those don't overlap. The more broadly you define where the publisher can sell your books, the more important it will be to you to have assurances that they will, in fact, do a great job in getting your book sold through those channels.

5. Options

The last aspect of the contract that should be of particular importance to you is the "options" or future rights clause. I've met many authors who thought they were signing a one book deal because the contract was, in fact, for just one book. What they didn't realize is that somewhere, buried in the bowels of the contract, was a clause that stated that the author was obligated to publish his or her next three books with that same publisher at the same terms of the agreement. This is commonly referred to as an option clause.

My recommendation is that, until you are confident that the publisher is the right publisher for you and does a very good job in publishing and working with you or partnering with you to sell your book, you may not want to grant to them the options for future books. And, if you do, you may want to have the opportunity to renegotiate new terms for the next contract.

A less restrictive way for you to show your publisher that you're committed to them without necessarily obligating you to them under any circumstance is to give them a right of first refusal. Depending upon how the language is worded, right of first refusal simply means that after you write your next book you agree to communicate with your present publisher and give them the opportunity to negotiate a fair contract with you. It doesn't mean that you have to work with them; it just means that you have to give them the opportunity to work with you.

Lastly, let me just say there can be all kinds of additional language in contracts that can be confusing and/or scary, but, in all likelihood, won't have much or any impact on the actual publication of your book or on your relationship with your publisher. It is important you have an understanding of what every part of your publishing contract means. If you aren't sure about something, feel free to call us. We're always happy to help you understand any ramifications of any publishing contract language.

CHAPTER 5

Getting the Content Right—How Your Book Reads

Once you have clear direction for your book, the next big step is actually getting it written. If you've already written your manuscript, or you are presently working on it, congratulations! It takes a great deal of determination and grit to go after the dream of writing your first book.

These days, being an accomplished writer (or even passing eighth grade English class), is not a prerequisite for becoming a published author. Oh sure, it helps, but your publisher should be able to advise you and provide competent editorial help to make your message read well and connect with your audience. In my experience, it's always better if the author puts the time and effort into writing their own book, even if they don't feel confident as a gifted communicator. The fact is, you have a certain way of thinking and speaking that will come through your writing and the very process of taking time to download your message onto paper (better yet, onto a Word document) will be a valuable experience for you. But, if you don't have time or the emotional energy to actually write your book, there are other ways to go about it.

Transcribe Voice Recordings

If you are already relaying your message to others in public speaking engagements, be certain to ask for a recording of each message. Later, you can have that message transcribed onto paper. The downside of this method is that you were presenting to a room full of people, and any experienced author will tell you that you write a book to one person—not an audience. To avoid the audience tone, you can choose to dictate your book directly into a handheld recorder and talk your way through the message. Manuscripts that are created from transcriptions ordinarily need a lot more editing, but often the convenience and time savings of getting a manuscript developed, even in rough form, is worth the extra editing it may require.

Ghostwriting

If you prefer to avoid writing the content of your book, you may choose to hire a ghostwriter. Publishers usually have a stable of professional ghostwriters that they call upon when they need a professional writer who will interview you to hear your heart and work with you to get your message developed. Sometimes a ghostwriter will use transcriptions of your speaking engagements or one-on-one voice recordings to help them capture your tone and style of speaking. Typically, a ghostwriter needs to talk to you and work out an outline for your book as well as get the necessary information that will ultimately become your book.

Ghostwriting services are not cheap. There is a wide range in pricing for ghostwriting services ranging from a few thousand dollars to in excess of one hundred thousand dollars. The more experience a ghostwriter has and the more bestsellers they've ghostwritten, the more expensive they will be.

Content Editing

Once you have a manuscript written, it's ready for editing. There are several stages or levels of editing. To keep things simple, I will summarize the basic kinds of editing you should be aware of: content editing, copy editing and proof editing. Don't assume that just because you have taken great pains to get your manuscript exactly the way you want it, that you don't need to have it edited. Every author needs an editor, and usually more than one!

It's important to understand that there is a wide range of levels of "content editing". A book edit can range from needing a rewrite to simply needing a line edit because the writing is tight and organized. Whatever editing your book receives, be grateful for it. It's important to be thick skinned and realize that a good editor is your friend and in the end, your book will be more readable and more marketable after their professional input. A very heavy content edit (sometimes called a rewrite edit or "book doctoring") is where the manuscript is in rough shape and major sections need to be shifted, deleted, added or reworked. A line edit is a very light content edit where the writing is clean and only a few minor changes in sentence structure or flow are required throughout the manuscript.

An experienced content editor is able to organize your thoughts and write fluently in such a way that your audience will grasp your points and hear your heart. A good content editor will be careful not to change words so that the manuscript still sounds like you. Keeping your "voice" is an important aspect of good publishing.

In my experience, a lot of first time authors think all that is necessary is a simple grammar check, when, in reality, the vast majority of manuscripts need a strong content edit. And you will need to brace yourself because your editor will have to do a lot of chopping of extraneous or repetitive material. They may have to come back to you to get additional illustrations and anecdotes to add color and depth to the work. In the end, you will be thrilled to see your important message reorganized into a flow of writing that speaks deeply to your readers.

Copy Editing

Look at it this way. Content editors worry about saying the right things. Copy editors worry about saying things right. Copy editing is focused solely on correcting grammar, syntax, spelling, fact checking, and looking for other possible errors that your English teacher would have found on your first research paper. The content editor will use proper English, but will be focused more on the organization and "readability" of your manuscript, not the technicalities of punctuation and spelling. The copy editor has an eagle eye for details and is extremely important in polishing the final presentation of your book. In essence, this editor will work on your book to clean up sentences, eliminate run on sentences, perhaps break up paragraphs, and do more work in helping fine-tune the readability of the manuscript.

Proof Editing

Proof editing is done after the manuscript has been laid out in its final interior design position. In other words, after the copy editor combs through the sentence structure and syntax of your book, your manuscript will be sent to a typesetter who will lay out the pages in a finished interior design. They'll make your manuscript look more like a book.

But whenever you manipulate pages of words and format them into a compelling design, the end result can look splotchy with odd looking sentences or other minor errors. The proof read is that one last look at the book before it goes to print, so it's important to have your book proof edited. It also provides that final level of fine tune corrections and an extra set of eyes to make sure all the previously noted copy edit corrections are made and see if any other minor mistakes need to be caught and corrected.

Author Review

Understand that whether your book goes through one level of editing or five, once you see your book in print, you will likely find errors. Hopefully not many, but you will find some. One way to avoid errors is to ask to look at your book after the copy editor and/or proofreader sees it. Editors, copy editors, proofreaders, and authors are all human and we are subject to error.

The more levels of editing involved, the more expensive it will be to publish your book. Most traditional publishers feel that three to five levels of edit are sufficient to get a book clean enough to take to market.

Be advised that many self-publishers do not allow for any level of editing in their basic publishing packages. If you decide to self-publish and want editing done to your manuscript (and you should), expect to pay extra for this service. Here's the rub. Most authors are not very objective in determining how much editing is really needed to make their manuscript sellable. You may think your manuscript reads just fine the way it is. But a professional publisher may feel that while your message is sound, it needs significant editing to make it marketable to the widest possible audience. My advice: be open to the input of your publisher on how much editing work will be needed.

Don't sweat it if after your book comes out, you find a typo here and there. Trust me; almost every New York Times best-selling book has errors in them. These can always be corrected at the next printing.

CHAPTER 6

Getting the Presentation Right—How Your Book Looks

How your message is presented will have a lot to do with how well it is received by your target audience. There are several components to a book that you should be familiar with and consider in bringing your message to the market.

Cover

The front cover of your book is arguably one of the most important marketing aspects of your book. It's what immediately jumps out and tells your perspective reader, "Hey, this is a message that will interest you!" It's important that your book be designed to appeal to your target audience. Don't succumb to the temptation of choosing a book cover design based primarily on what you prefer. Your tastes may not be the same as the audience you want to reach!

Publishers are experienced in designing covers that grab the attention of readers, so take their input seriously. Trade sales teams present books to retail book buyers on a regular basis. These book buyers make their living deciding what books will appeal to their book buying audience. Buyers and publishers alike are not always right, but they are still the gatekeepers that determine which books get placed on store shelves and which books don't. I know they say you can't judge a book by its cover, but book buyers do this every day, at least in part. Even if your book is going to be primarily sold in venues other than a bookstore or on-line store, how the book looks and what is said on the cover matters a great deal.

The central components of the cover are:

1. Title
2. Subtitle
3. Cover Design
4. Endorsements
5. Bullet Points
6. Back cover copy
7. ISBN and BISAC codes

In general, you want the title of your book to be either very clear and specific in defining what your book is about, or it should be very engaging, compelling and clever. If you have a book title that is clever, but not particularly clear, then it will be important that your subtitle gives a clear explanation of the benefit received. For example, if your book title is *Lose 10 Pounds in 10 Days*, that is specific enough that your subtitle becomes less important. However, if the title of your book is *Take the 10 Day Challenge* or *10 Days to a New You*, in that case, the title is interesting, maybe even compelling, but it doesn't tell the reader much on what the book is about. It would be important to have a subtitle that is more specific. It is always important that your cover design be appealing to your target audience and enhance and support the words on the cover. For example, if your audience is educated and sophisticated, you may want to go for a clean, simple design. Or, it's possible that your audience may be just the right crowd for a much more garish, bright, and bold cover design. A good cover designer will be aware of these things and want to know as much as possible about your target audience and your message before they can come up with an effective cover design that will appeal to that audience as well as align with your message.

Endorsements

Endorsements add credibility to your message and to you as the author. You should always seek strong endorsements for your book. Here's why. You are asking a complete stranger to be willing to pay money to read what you have to say. An endorsement acts like a favorable movie review in that it lets potential readers feel better about investing in what you have to say without having any personal track record with you as an author. Endorsements can be published in the beginning pages of your book, on the back cover of your book or on the front cover. Putting an endorsement on the cover of your book only makes sense when the person endorsing the book is widely recognized or well known by your target audience.

Bullet Points

Often times, it's beneficial to have additional benefit statements about what your book offers the reader listed right on the front cover. Think about most magazine covers, how they feature several different articles found in that particular issue. Bullet points listed on the cover of your book serve to let a prospective reader get more of a sense of what helpful benefit they can expect to receive from reading your book. For example, in our dieting book illustration, you might have bullet points on the front or back cover that say,

- Learn how to satisfy your sweet tooth while still cutting down on sugar

- Why most diets don't work, but this one will

- Discover the missing ingredient that has kept you from achieving your weight goals!

Each of these statements is designed to draw the reader in and make them more and more interested in picking up the book and consider purchasing it.

Back Cover Copy

Use the back page of your book cover or dust jacket to give a prospective reader a short and enticing summary of not just what your book is about, but how your book will help and benefit the reader. Take time to work with a professional copywriter or marketing expert to get this copy crafted well. If done correctly, the paragraph or two that you spend on the back cover will be the most compelling description of your book found anywhere. In fact, much of your marketing promotional copy can be adapted from the back cover copy written.

You may choose to allow space to tell about yourself in a brief author bio. Here again, be selective in what you say about yourself. Readers don't necessarily want to get to know you as much as they want to see why you are qualified to write this book. Craft your author bio with this in mind.

ISBN and BISAC Codes

ISBN stands for International Standard Book Number. This number, when coupled with a correlating bar code, is essential in allowing retailers to scan and track book sales through their inventory management systems. The ISBN number is typically purchased by your publisher through RR Bowker Company. The BISAC code stands for Book Industry Standards and Communications. Essentially, this number is what bookstores use to determine where to place your book on their shelves. Is this a travel book? A self-help book? A cookbook? There are three parts to the BISAC code. We don't need to get into much detail on this other than to say, you should be clear about the appropriate categories into which your book falls and list a BISAC code that accurately reflects those categories.

Copyright Page

This is the page that makes your book look professional to libraries, bookstores, and readers. There are many variations of what's included here, but these are the basics that every copyright page should include. The book title, subtitle, and author name, the publishing company's name, contact information and website, the year of publication, the copyright notice and statement, the critically important ISBN and the specific edition or reprint number of this particular edition.

You may choose to add acknowledgments of those who helped develop the book such as the editor, cover designer who provided any photographs, and any other disclaimers that you may wish to add, but these are not required.

Half Title Page

This is sometimes called the "Master Title". This page carries nothing but the main title, centered in the beginning of the page, and nothing but the title of the book. Most publications without a half title just look wrong. This tradition is said to go back to the earliest days of book manufacturing when printed books were stored as printed sheets. If a customer wanted the book, he purchased it and arranged for his own personal hand binding. The first page on the folded sheet was the title page and it was at risk of getting dirty or torn, so early publishers initiated the practice of placing the half page title on the top; a page that was nice yet dispensable.

Title Page

The title page is usually the first page you see after the half title page, inside the front book cover. The title page carries the title of the book, the subtitle, the author, and the name of the publisher.

Dedication Page

This is a place where, if you choose to, you may acknowledge the person or group that most inspired you or led you to writing this book or supported you throughout the book's development. You do not need to thank every contributor to your book. You will have room to do that on the acknowledgment page. The dedication is optional and not a requirement, but it gives the reader an idea of who's important in your life and shows gratitude to the people who influenced you most or cheered you on throughout your book writing process.

Preface

The preface is where you, the author, talk directly to the reader to give them information they need to know before reading the book. Sometimes this page will reveal how the idea for your book was developed. A preface is used more commonly in nonfiction than fiction. The preface is usually signed and sometimes dated by the author. Again, a preface is not necessarily required.

Prologue

Prologues are usually used most often in fiction. A prologue describes the events that occurred before and, occasionally, during the heart of the story. It is the background information that helps the reader to understand certain aspects of the story they're about to read.

Foreword

A foreword is a special kind of introduction that offers supportive information relative to the book. It is always written by another person other than the author; preferably someone who is well known or highly credentialed, or considered of good reputation.

Acknowledgments

The acknowledgments page(s) allow you to thank the people who are in some way relevant to the book. Acknowledgments may include your publisher, the editor at the publishing house, the author's agent, a supportive spouse, etc. The acknowledgment page sometimes follows the dedication page, the Table of Contents, or can even appear in the back page of the book, depending on the publisher's preference.

Introduction

The introduction essentially tells the reader two things—how they can expect to benefit from reading this book and a bit of background as to why you decided to write this book. Most fiction books do not have an introduction, but they may include a prologue.

In nonfiction books, the introduction may be an informal 'Dear Reader' letter, getting the reader excited about the information they are about to experience, as well as, giving an overview of the book's contents. Typically, the numbering of the book starts at the introduction.

Table of Contents (TOC)

The Table of Contents is simply a general outline of the organization of your nonfiction book. Most of the time, a fiction book will not list its chapters within a TOC. In nonfiction books, however, the chapter titles will be listed with the pages on which they begin. As a general rule, it's helpful to have chapter titles that are informative or some-times clever and engaging. Think about somebody who doesn't know what your book is about and they flip to the Table of Contents. Will reading the chapter titles make them curious? Will they make the reader want to explore the book further?

Footnotes or Endnotes

Footnotes are typically small notations at the bottom of each page that reference certain documents or source material that was mentioned on that page. Endnotes are normally referenced within the book and sourced in detail at the end of each chapter or in the back matter of your book. If these source documents are listed at the end of the chapter or the end of the book, then they're referred to as 'endnotes' rather than footnotes. Whether you choose to site your sources as footnotes or endnotes is a personal preference.

Epilogue

An epilogue is a final chapter at the end of a story that often serves to reveal the fates of the characters that were referenced in the book, especially in the case of fiction or a personal true to life story such as a memoir, biography, or autobiography. Some epilogues may feature scenes only tangentially related to the subject or story. They can be used to hint at a sequel or to wrap up all the loose ends. They can occur at a significant period of time after the main plot has ended. In some cases, the epilogue has been used to give the main character a chance to "speak freely". An epilogue can continue in the same narrative style and perspective as the preceding story, although the form of an epilogue can be drastically different from the rest of the story. When an author steps in and speaks directly to the reader, it is more properly considered an afterword. It can also be used as a sequel.

Binding

Another thing to consider in publishing your book is how you want the book bound. The two most common formats for printed books are: trade paper perfect-bound (paperback) or hard case binding and dust jacket (hardback). Paperback books are typically black and white text wrapped around a heavier stock of paper printed in full color with a square back binding known as "perfect binding". Paperback books are typically less expensive than hardback books. Hardback books can be the exact same size and same interior as a paperback book, but, instead of having a paper cover, they have a thick sheet of cardboard wrapped in paper or cloth with a foil imprint on the spine and sometimes also on the cover. In most cases, a hardback book has a separate full color sheet wrapped around it, referred to as a dust jacket. Hardback books may retail from $5–$10 per book more than the same book released as a paperback. As a result, publishers usually reserve hardbacks for titles that are either:

1. Published by a very well-known or respected author.

2. The information is considered exclusive and/
or more "valuable" and, therefore, can carry
a higher price than a hardback brings.

Authors often want their book to be in hardback because of the perceived higher quality, but know your audience. You don't want to price your book out of the reach or interest of your audience.

Trim Size

The typical trim size of a standard trade paperback or hardback book can vary. It used to be that books were always published in a standard size, and that is 6" x 9". Now, however, publishers experiment with a variety of trim sizes from 5" x 7" to 5½" x 8½", 6" x 9", and any number of subtle variations in between. Sometimes, a book may initially be released in hardback in a full 6" x 9" size and then, later, released in a paperback edition in either 6" x 9" or slightly smaller, 5½" x 8½". Fiction books, especially, may later be released in what is referred to as mass market or mass merchandise size, which is most commonly 4¼" x 7¼". As you might expect, the retail price of books vary both on their binding and their size so that hardback books typically retail from $19.99–$24.99 and paperback books typically retail for $12.99–$16.99, and mass merchandise books typically retail from $7.99–$12.99.

As you might imagine, all these decisions about how your book should look should be made with the end goal of seeing your book get into the hands of the most number of readers possible. But, while all our discussions have been based on a printed book, know that there are many other formats in which your message may be presented.

CHAPTER 7

Packaging Your Message

As you develop your message, it's important to think about in what formats your target audience will most appreciate receiving your message. Don't assume a "one size fits all" mindset when it comes to getting your message into the hands of readers. Know your target audience. Know their lifestyles; know how they live and what packaging or presentations will be most helpful for them. You may love the feel of a printed book in your hand and, therefore, want to see your message developed as a trade paper or hardback book. Fine, but consider that your target audience may best be able to receive and benefit from your message in one of these other formats besides a printed book.

E-books

E-books, (short for electronic books), is one of the fastest growing segments of the publishing world. For example, the Association of American Publishers reports that statistics show a triple digit growth (+$150.7 M) for e-books in the religious genre. An electronic book is just what it says. It's your book's message stored digitally instead of printed on paper. It reads just the same as a printed book and depending on the e-reader you use (tablet or smart phone), you can literally turn pages by simply scrolling your finger across the screen. Amazon Kindle was one of the first in the market with e-books and is still the most popular provider of e-book formats. Apple, through their iPhone and iPad, provide e-reading formats, as well as Barnes & Noble's Nook format. E-books have the potential to not only include the text of your message, but also provide links to websites, photos, music, even videos. While e-books are not yet as prevalent as printed books, sales of e-books are out-pacing their printed cousins.

Magazine Articles

I see many authors so enamored with writing a book that they over-write. In general, people today are busy so it's often helpful to have your message presented in the shortest way possible. For example, if you can present your message in a 1,500–2,500 word magazine article, why not do that? There's no point in stretching your point into a 35,000–55,000 word book manuscript if you can communicate your central points in much fewer words. Some messages need time to be unpacked and so a book is much better than a blog or magazine article—but sometimes not.

On the other hand, publishers or writers sometimes take excerpts or adaptations of their book and submit them as magazine articles as a way of enticing readers to go further by ordering a book after reading the initial magazine article.

Audio Books

How many times have you seen somebody jogging along the sidewalk or working out at the gym while listening to their headphones? For those who have a 30 minute or longer commute to work, an audio book format is often the most desirable.

Mobile App

Imagine taking your book and adding videos, adding other supplemental material to it and developing it into a more robust, interactive format. Say you've written a cookbook. In addition to including the recipes, why not include a short video of you actually making the dish? Or perhaps, show photos of the dish presented in multiple ways? You may include separate ingredient listings or alternative ingredients that could be substituted. Why not invite readers to rate a dish or make comments via your app? This would give a more interactive reader experience. And the more you can interact with your readers, the more likely they are to become "raving fans".

Perhaps you've written a book on finances. In addition to the text of your book, you could include a mortgage calculator in your app, or a way to project how much money a person will spend on interest by plugging in the interest rate and term of the loan. You might provide links to sponsoring investment firms you recommend and you could charge those organizations a fee to be included in your mobile app! The possibilities are endless.

Consider mobile apps as an e-book on steroids.

As tablet readers and smart phones become more prevalent and the technology that drives them becomes more and more affordable, we are seeing the traditional e-book (which is just an electronic version of a printed book) now offering more features including full color photos and graphics, web links and even video clips. At this point, the e-book starts to look and act more like a mobile website or a true mobile app.

A mobile website is just that—a website that can be accessed from your smart phone or tablet, saved with a bookmark/icon so it looks just like a true mobile app. But, here's the difference. A true mobile app has software integrated into it, so that when downloaded into a device, it can open and operate regardless of whether there is internet service available. A mobile website, on the other hand, can only be opened and operate where the device can access the internet. Think of it this way. If you store a Word document on your computer's hard drive, you can access that document anywhere you choose to turn on your computer. But, if that Word document is stored on a cloud server, then you can only access that Word document if your computer can connect to the internet.

Small Group/Curriculum Resource

Many times, the message of a book can be best absorbed if it's done in a group setting or in a more interactive way. Consider taking your message and adding study questions at the end or adding a companion workbook to go along with the message of your book and creating a series of short, introductory videos where you, as the author, or perhaps another on-camera spokesperson, provide video summaries of each chapter of the book. This allows the reader to both see and hear your message, then engage in discussion with others or possibly enter in a workbook setting with your message. A small group resource can be an even more effective way to present your message than just a book.

Online Courses

Similar to a curriculum or small group resource, an online course provides a more interactive way for readers to review, read, watch, or listen to your message and then engage, think about, and/or respond to the message, while engaging with you online. The important thing is that each of these formats provides an additional way for your message to be embraced.

Pace Your Message and Consider How to Expand Your Packaging

Think about the pacing of your message. Often times, I talk with authors who have a particular message that has powerfully impacted their life or they have a specific skill they want to share with their audience. They feel the need to tell their audience everything they know about a subject in one book. This seldom works and can be overwhelming. Think about your book as a tool to motivate and inspire people for change and let the book then lead people into a more interactive and expanded format to apply that information that you're sharing in their lives.

For example, Robert Kiyosaki wrote a book called *Rich Dad, Poor Dad* that challenged readers with the concept that there is a different way to invest and build wealth than to go to college, get a job, and work hard. The book didn't tell you how to invest your money, but it inspired the reader to think that there are different ways to invest money and to build wealth that will take them further. Many people who read the book signed up for one of Robert's self-help courses or wealth-development courses. They spent more money on those courses, because the interactive resources or online courses were a better format for the reader to more fully engage with his message. Kiyosaki made more money and his readers got more value. Everybody wins.

The same thing can hold true with diet and exercise books. Bill Phillips wrote a book called *Body for Life*. It didn't tell you exactly how to lose a ton of weight and look great in a bathing suit or bikini. But it made you want to lose weight, made you believe that you could lose weight, and inspired in the reader's mind that Phillips had the secret to actually experience the kind of success he was showing you in his book. From there, many thousands of people signed up for his *Body for Life* program that included workout videos, workbooks, menus, etc. In other words, the purpose of the book was not to tell the reader every-thing that Bill Phillips knew about losing weight; it was to motivate readers to connect with Bill further in purchasing interactive resources from him.

An IRS tax specialist might write a book that gives you hope that you can break free from your IRS problems. Hopefully that book will inspire you to sign up for his IRS problem-solver course and, depending on the severity of your problem, may lead you to actually hire the tax specialist to solve your IRS problems for you.

As you can see, a book can be the top of a funnel that leads readers to a deeper interactive online or small group course that leads some readers to personally hire you for more individual training.

It's important to think through how your message can best be packaged, and the different ways it can be packaged, to have the highest impact on the stronger number of people.

CHAPTER 8

Sales Channels
for Your Book

Most people assume that to sell a book, you simply have to get it into the bookstores. Case closed...let the fat royalty checks start rolling in! Nothing can be further from the truth. Even if your book was stacked three copies deep in every bookstore in the country, what would make people come into the store to look for your title? Do you think that just because your book is on the store shelf, it will sell? I hope through reading this chapter you will expand your thinking and vision for all the ways that you can help get your book into the hands of the readers who most want and need to read what you have to say.

In general, there are four major ways or channels that books are sold (book stores being one of them). It will be important for you to make sure that you have considered how to maximize sales of your book in each of these four channels:

1. Trade sales

2. Event sales
3. Internet sales
4. Specialty sales

Trade Sales

Bookstore sales are what most authors covet and, to be honest, they are the hardest sales to attain. When I refer to trade sales, I'm referring to books that are sold through traditional bookselling retail outlets and the distributors who service those accounts. We'll talk more specifically about trade sales in chapter ten. Because there are so many new books published every year, most retailers can't easily keep up with ordering titles from so many different publishers, so they will often order book titles from multiple publishers through a single distributor.

Distributors play a middle man role in the book distribution process. There are about a million new titles being published each year. Rather than having to keep open accounts with every publisher, a bookstore buyer will simply order book titles they want to carry from one distributor who in turn will order those titles from the various publishers who produced them. It's only when a book starts selling significantly well that the book buyer may choose to order that particular title directly from the publisher in order to pick up a slightly better discount than what they get from their distributor.

It's very difficult for an individual author to establish an account with a distributor or major book store chain. The one notable exception to this is Amazon.com. Amazon is willing to work directly with individual authors, but most of the other bookstores, distributors, book clubs, libraries and rack-jobbers in the sales channel, commonly referred to as "the trade", only want to deal with a recognized publisher who will produce anywhere from ten to one thousand titles per year. While you may choose to work as an author on your own, it is generally in your best interest to find a publishing house or trade distribution company to represent your title to the bookstores and other trade accounts. This is not only because it's difficult to get into the stores, but also because someone has to invoice the stores, collect money, follow up to ensure stores are adhering to your trade policies and handle any returns that are sent back because after ordering your book, the stores realized that all the copies they ordered haven't sold… so they simply return the books to the publisher for a full credit! Handling trade sales is just a lot more work than the typical author wants to get into managing.

Event Sales

Any time you are asked to speak to a group, perhaps as a workshop leader or key note speaker, you have the opportunity to speak about the topic of your book. The people who hear you speak should all be highly motivated to buy a copy of your book because your talk has encouraged and inspired them to learn more about what you have to say. You should always plan to have your book available for sale at any event where you speak, present or exhibit. This can take a little coordination on your part to make sure books get sent to the venues where you are present and there are people there to man the tables, collect the money, and record the sales, etc., but it's well worth it. The ones most motivated to buy your book will be the ones who just heard you speak on the topic of your book. Event sales are typically the most profitable sales for an author.

In addition to the direct book sales you make at an event, it's always a good idea to collect contact information, especially e-mail addresses, of all the people who heard you speak and add them to your mailing list.

It's best to reduce the price of your book slightly to even dollar amounts when you sell at events so you don't have to make change. For example, a $15.95 book you might choose to sell at your event for $15.00 or 2 for $25.00.

Internet Sales

Internet sales are any book sales made as a result of driving people to your website to click the "buy now" button to order your book. The beauty of internet sales is the internet provides you with so many different ways to capture the attention of the prospective buying audience and point them to your website to order your book. For example, you might do an e-blast or blog or get other bloggers to write about your book (a Blog Tour) or you might post comments about or from your book on your Facebook or Twitter accounts. You might make short video trailers about the message of your book to run on YouTube. In short, use the internet and social media opportunities to make potentially millions of people aware of what you have to say through your book and provide those people with compelling reasons to go to your website where they can simply click and order the book.

As a general rule, internet marketing is very inexpensive, but it does take some time and expertise to do it well.

Specialty Sales

Specialty sales can be highly lucrative, however, specialty sales can be difficult to describe. The kind of specialty sales opportunities you have will depend widely on the type of message you have to share.

For example, say you've written a book on how to improve your golf swing. Selling your book in a golf pro shop or at charity golf tournaments is an obvious opportunity. Since golf pro shops aren't primarily book stores, selling to pro shops would be considered a specialty sale. If you've written a book on homeopathic remedies for common ailments, you might find that health food stores would love to carry that book. If you set up a table or booth at the local farmer's market, you may find yourself in front of a ready and eager audience to buy your book. Both venues would be potentially great places to sell your book and fall under "specialty sales".

Some of the most lucrative specialty sales opportunities involve partnering with other organizations to purchase large quantities of your book at significant discounts. For example, let's say you're a guest on a particular talk show to talk about your weight loss program and that talk show wants to offer your book to their viewers for a special price or, if it's a nonprofit funded organization, such as NPR or Trinity Broadcast Network, they may choose to offer your book to their donors for a financial gift or contribution to the organization. There are many other specialty sales opportunities. Let's say you have written a book to encourage women to find life after divorce; you might find certain women's groups or self-help/ recovery groups interested in buying your books by the 100's, even 1,000's, at a significant discount so that their members can offer your book as fundraising gift. Perhaps you've written a book to motivate people to be their best on the job and you find employers that would like to offer a copy to each of their employees. If you get one large company with 1,500 employees to buy your book to give away as a gift to their employees, that can be a significant sale for you.

Consider all of the direct marketing companies that have large numbers of affiliates who attend motivational conferences. If you could get your book sold to those organizations, it could be worth thousands of dollars and possibly generate thousands or even tens of thousands of book sales for you. The most important thing to think about is where your most likely reader (those people who will become your "raving fans") can be reached and how you can get your book in front of them.

One final note—sales of your book is really up to YOU, not your publisher.

It's good to remember that, while your publisher can probably best help you with the trade sales, the other three sources are probably best managed by you, as the author, and are far more profitable. Many authors assume that once they have a publisher, they can sit back and relax. The truth is you have to plan on being the dominant cheerleader and marketer for your book.

Consider this formula. If you sell 100 books at Barnes & Noble's, by the time the publisher pays the appropriate discount to the retail chain and their distributor (typically about 50%) and then pays a royalty percentage on those sales, there's not much left over for you, maybe less than a dollar a book! But, when you sell those same 100 copies through your website directly or at an event where you speak, you get to keep all the revenue, less whatever the book cost you.

Barnes & Nobles' Sales 100 copies x $15 x 50% = $750 x 15% royalty =	$112.50
Vs.	
100 copies x $15 on your website— cost per book at $5.00 =	$1,000.00

As you can see, you will do much better selling the books yourself, even factoring in what those books cost you.

Get out your publishing playbook and lay out your sales and marketing strategies for each of the four sales channels discussed in this chapter. If you need help putting together this strategy, don't hesitate to call us. This is what we do and we love to help authors figure out creative ways to get their books in front of the readers who will benefit most.

CHAPTER 9

Marketing Your Book— How to Get Started

As I mentioned in the last chapter, there are about one million new book titles released every year. Amazing, huh? So how are you going to make your book stand out, get noticed, and get into the hands of your intended readers? The people you want to reach are busy. They've got a lot on their minds and a ton of pressures, issues and activities competing for their attention. You're sitting there with a message you believe will be of interest to them. But how do you get their attention? And once you have their attention, how are you, in a matter of seconds, going to convince them that what you have to say is actually worth paying for? You've heard of the 80/20 rule? I think writing your book represents only 20% of your work. Book marketing, publicity and promotion represent the other 80%! It takes diligent and strategic effort to get your book published and sold. But it is not a mountain you can't climb.

The place to start is to develop a marketing strategy. Take time to prepare a thoughtful, well-researched document

that outlines what you plan to do and the results you anticipate receiving from your efforts. Be specific in setting goals.
Remember, you can't manage what you can't measure. For
example, don't write down "Contact my past clients and
ask them to buy a copy." A more measurable approach
would be to say "Contact 150 past clients by June 21. Make
400 attempts, 150 connections and sell 2000 copies at an
average of $8.50 per book." Now you have something more
specific to which you can hold yourself accountable, and
know whether you exceeded or fell short of your marketing
and sales projections.

A sound marketing strategy involves these components:

- Identify your target audience (IDENTIFY)

- Figure out how to reach them (CONNECT)

- Get noticed by them (AWARENESS)

- Present them with the right offer with the
  right call to action (MOTIVATE)

- Catch them with the right timing and
  frequency (FREQUENCY)

Ten Marketing Principles

As you begin planning your marketing strategy, here are ten basic principles to keep in mind:

1. Word of Mouth is still the best form of marketing. Think about what you can do to get people talking about your book. You need to create a buzz so that people will tell their friends, family, and coworkers about your book. Of course, the most essential key to this is having a good book, well written, on a topic that is of interest to your target audience. No amount of money or clever marketing can make up for a message that simply doesn't connect with the intended reader. Assuming your book is on point, there are several things you can do to encourage word of mouth advertising. Start by simply asking people to tell their friends. Ask them in the back of your book. Ask them on your social networks. Offer contests and incentives to get people to "spread the word".

2. Marketing takes time. Determine right now that you will do something every day for a full year to market your book. Many New York Times best-selling authors, who are now with a traditional publisher, started out self-publishing or working with a collaborative publisher and slowly built a following through their own efforts.

3. Make sure all your marketing focuses not on the content of your book, but what your book will do for the reader. Benefits sell product over features. Let your readers know how your book will make their life better in some way. What is your "value proposition"? This harkens back to one of the five key questions asked back in Chapter Three. Make sure in all your marketing you clearly answer the "what's in it for me" question.

4. Do whatever it takes to get noticed, to stand out. Seth Godin, in his bestselling book *The Purple Cow,* talks about the importance of doing something unique and different to stand out from the crowd. If you've written a book about transitions in life, what are you going to do to get noticed by your audience—the people who are currently going through those transitions and need what you have to say. Remember, we are all way too busy and inherently skeptical. To grab your reader's attention, you have to do or say something that is unique and compelling—yet believable—to get noticed.

5. Always have a call to action. I come from a direct marketing background and learned early on in my career that a key to a successful promotion is giving your customer a reason to respond NOW, not later...because if they don't respond now, when you have their attention, they likely never will. Always have incentives for the reader to show the advantage they will have if they call or click to order your book right on the spot.

6. You can't manage what you can't measure. When crafting your marketing strategy, be specific in identifying your strategy to generate book sales in each of the four channels of sales we discussed in the last chapter. It may be that for you, most of your focus will be on only one or two of those four channels. That's OK. But for each channel of sales, outline, in as much detail as you can, what you will do to generate sales, what you will spend and how many books you expect to sell as a result of your efforts. Don't be shy in setting out specific sales goals you expect to see from your efforts. Always be willing to adapt. Drop the promotions that aren't bearing fruit and do more of what is working well.

7. Don't be timid in asking for an order. I run into authors all the time who somehow feel that it is arrogant or conceited to promote their own book. They don't feel comfortable asking people to pay money to purchase what they have to say. But I say you should be the most passionate and authentic cheerleader for your message possible. Of course, you don't want to be obnoxious about it. But, for goodness sake, if you don't believe that your message is worth reading, then why should anyone else? Remember, you wrote your book to help people, to benefit them in some way. Promoting your book is not about you. It's not about lining your pockets; it's about bringing value and benefit to someone else. When this is your motivation, people will sense that.

8. Start early in building your own database. A key to any successful marketing campaign is getting your message in front of your target audience as many times and in as many ways as possible. How do you do that? The best place to start is by leveraging the relationships you already have. Think about every school you attended, every club and association you belong to, every client you've ever served, every contact in your email files and company database. Maybe none of these people are prospective readers of your book, but perhaps they represent access to a segment of your target audience. Your marketing campaign shouldn't be limited to just asking these people to buy a copy of your book, (though it could be). Your marketing strategy should be about getting these people to, in some way, promote, endorse, excerpt, distribute, review or sell your book *to the people they influence.*

9. Ask more than once. Part of any marketing strategy involves getting in front of your target audience often enough (frequency), in the right way and in the proper timing. For example, you may have an amazing Christmas Devotional that your target audience would love. But if they are presented the opportunity to purchase your book in July, or perhaps right after they had to pay for an unexpected auto repair, it won't matter if you had a brilliant offer that was compellingly presented. You just caught them at the wrong time. You want to allow for enough frequency for your promotions to get results. Sometimes people need to hear about a message several times before they finally decide to buy.

10. Always sell one reader at a time. It's easy to slip into the habit of talking to your audience as a group, as the huge mass of followers that you truly hope to attract. But making a buying decision is a singular experience. In all your promotions, talk to one person. Make your promotional copy personal. The more effectively you can write and talk to one person, and make each person reading, hearing or experiencing your promotion feel as if you are talking just to them, the more effective you will be.

I realize that everything I've shared with you in this chapter is a general principle. The fact is it takes time to outline all the specific examples and creative ways that your particular message can be marketed. Please feel free to contact us for more personal help in crafting your book marketing plan. It's what we love to do.

CHAPTER 10

Your Trade Sales Strategy

In chapter eight, I mentioned the four main sales channels for your book. Let's talk for a moment about trade sales. For most, trade sales will not be the most effective or profitable channel of sales—but seeing their book in the bookstores and on-line is what every author wants.

Trade sales are sales of your book made to sales outlets whose primary focus is book sales. These include:

- Independent bookstores—Typically 1–15 stores privately owned, most often, in one region of the country.

- Store chains—Typically owned by a larger corporation and might have 15–1500 stores (Barnes & Noble, Books-A-Million, Family Christian Stores, Lifeway Stores, etc.).

- Distributors—These are organizations that act as a middle-man in the bookselling process. Since most bookstores don't want to keep track of the thousands of authors and publishers, they will order multiple books from one distributor who in turn will deal with those hundreds, if not thousands, of smaller publishers and individual authors.

- Rack-Jobbers—This is a company that sets up a small display, usually a spinner rack to sell a collection of books, sometimes of a particular genre, such as "Inspirational reading" or "Business topics" in a retail outlet other than a bookstore. This could be a grocery store, drugstore, convenience store, etc.

- Book Clubs—You may have seen these advertised in magazines. A book club selects books to feature to their members who pay a fee and receive a book a month or similar.

- Libraries—can be both public and private. Libraries buy a lot of books and are often overlooked by many authors and publishers.

- On-Line retailers—Amazon.com is the most recognized, but most bookstore chains also have their own on-line bookselling presence.

- Big Box Stores—these are large wholesale stores such as Walmart, Target, Costco, etc. that sell books as part of their overall product mix.

In most cases, these trade sales accounts are not set up to deal with individual authors so you will need a publisher to help make sure your book is available to be sold in any of these trade sales channels. Amazon is the one notable exception. They sell millions of books every year and they are the one major trade account that will sell books directly from authors. Even so, if you have the opportunity to work with a publisher, you will likely experience better sales results working with a publisher who has an established account with Amazon.

In selling books in the trade, there are some key principles to be aware of.

1. Recognize that, with rare exception, the buyers in all of the above categories don't care a lick about your message. What they care about is whether your book will sell more copies than the next book. No matter how wonderful, helpful or inspiring your message is, don't take this personally, but just know that a book buyer simply doesn't care. Telling a buyer about the wonder of your message is wasted breath. What they want to know is what are you going to do to drive more traffic to their store or site than the next author?

2. Every sale you make to a trade account is essentially a consignment sale, meaning that it's returnable. So don't get too excited about seeing a store chain place an order for 500 copies of your book. Get excited when they reorder! Because if they reorder, that means the first 500 copies you sold them are moving well enough that their inventory controls are indicating they need to order more. If you make a sale to a trade account, they can typically take up to six months to sell the book and even then, decide if the books haven't all sold, to return to you the copies that didn't sell.

3. Trade accounts mostly care about new titles. With so many new books coming out every year, it's next to impossible to interest a trade buyer to consider ordering a book that's already been out on the market. There are exceptions to this. But this explains why most traditional publishers, who tend to rely most heavily on trade sales to sell copies of their book, invest any marketing dollars they choose to spend within the first six months of a new title's release. Their sales team will work hard to convince buyers to order in a new title and then cross their fingers that those initial orders "sell through" to actual customers at the retail level. Otherwise, the retail accounts will likely just return the unsold copies for a full refund from the publisher. And just to be clear, unless you are already a best-selling author, don't count on your publisher investing any marketing dollars on your book beyond some basic in-house efforts. It just doesn't happen, or not very often.

4. Trade accounts typically want a 6-month lead window. What this means is that once you have a cover design for your book, you or your publisher will want to present your book to the key buyers in order to get them to agree to order in your book. In almost any retail industry, there are people whose job it is to determine which products the retailer will carry. If you sell ties, there are "tie buyers" who evaluate which styles, colors and manufacturers from whom they want to order product. The book industry is no different. A large retailer will have several buyers who each specialize in a particular genre of books. For example, a children's book buyer will focus on getting to know what's new in children's book products, what topics parents are interested in, what age-range seems to be selling the most, etc. A fiction buyer wants to know what type of fiction is selling these days and look for fiction titles they believe will sell the best in their stores.

Buyers who are presented a new title in March expect that the book will be available to sell between September and November.

In working with the Trade, here are some key terms to be aware of:

Publication Date or Street Date—This is the date that your book is expected to be on the store shelves and available for customers to purchase.

Release Date—This is typically the date your book is available from your printer or your warehouse to be shipped to the bookstores or distributors. The release date is usually about six weeks prior to the street or "Pub" date. This allows time for books to be shipped to the retailer and time for the retailer to inventory the title, sticker (if necessary) and get the book properly stocked on the shelves.

Note, if you self-publish or work with a collaborative publisher, you can typically get copies of your books published and printed more quickly than working with a traditional publisher. Therefore, it would be wise to establish a pub date for your book somewhat later than the date by when you anticipate receiving your author copies for direct sales through your non-trade sales channels.

Sales Tip Sheet (STS)—This is a 1–2 page document that book buyers want to see in order to quickly decide whether or not they want to carry your book on their shelves. The STS typically shows a picture of the cover of your book, summarizes the central benefit of the book, defines who is the most likely reader, may reference other comparative titles, tells the specifications of the book such as the ISBN #, page count, binding type, retail price, BISAC Code (Book Industry Standards and Communications Code), the formats in which the book is available, and perhaps most importantly, outlines what type of marketing and promotion will be done to drive traffic to their store and generate sales. **If your publisher is not creating a sales tip sheet and personally presenting that to key buyers, don't count on getting much, if any, trade sales.**

Advance Review Copies (ARC's)—The second key tool in a trade sales strategy is an advance review copy (ARC). These are bound copies of your edited and typeset book, sent to key industry reviewers. Book buyers want all the help they can get in determining which new titles released every year they should consider carrying or promoting. If your book has gotten positive industry reviews, the buyer will have more interest and confidence in ordering your book.

My philosophy about trade sales is simple. Bookstores don't generate demand for your book…you do that through your direct sales and marketing strategy. Bookstores are reactionary. They don't (for the most part) promote a title or create a bestseller. They will, however, help you become a bestselling author in that they can help ensure that your book is easily available to purchase through their outlets. But unless you are doing something in the media to create awareness and drive people into the stores or on-line to order your book, even if your book is actively stocked and presented, that will not translate into lots of trade sales for you. Plan on having a trade sales strategy; just don't rely on the trade to be what drives sales of your book.

.

CHAPTER 11

Your Direct Sales Strategy

If trade sales is not going to be the engine that drives in sales of your book, then what does? The short answer is YOU! Determine right now that you are going to be the principle cheerleader and sales promoter of your book. If you do this, you will likely be more tired, but much happier about the results! I want to quickly review what we touched on in chapter eight. Besides trade sales, there are three main ways you can sell your book directly:

1. Through the internet
2. At events where you speak
3. Through specialty sales outlets you set up.

I could write an entire book about each of these three marketing and sales channels. But rather than overwhelm you, allow me to give you a simple overview and perhaps a few keys to effectively selling your book through these three direct sales channels. Understand that HigherLife is happy to help craft a detailed and customized marketing strategy for each of these channels. Just call us for a free marketing consultation. We'd be happy to help.

Event Sales Marketing

Probably the most profitable source of book sales will come from personal events where you are present as a speaker and/ or exhibitor. When you speak at a conference or seminar or any other type of public event, make sure that your topic is aligned with the message of your book. When you do this, your talk becomes a compelling factor in making people want to buy your book. Think of your talk as an "infomercial" for your book. People will hopefully be motivated by what you have to say, but the real impact comes when they decide to act on whatever it is you share. So, having your book in their hands to read, ponder and respond to will actually help solidify the message you initially presented at your event.

Here are a few keys to maximizing book sales at events.

1. Stack 'em High, and Watch 'em Buy. It's an old adage, but it works. Have several large stacks of books out on the table for display and you will sell more copies than if you only have a few copies nicely fanned out on display.

2. Always sell your book for an even dollar amount. People don't want to make change. If possible, have the amount be a discount off the retail price of your book.

3. Offer a no-risk or money back guarantee. Most people will never take you up on it, but just offering it conveys confidence and will ease a consumer's insecurity about buying something new they don't know much about or have never tried before.

4. Make it easy for people to buy. Offer credit card processing if you can. There are scanners available that plug right into your smart phone that turn your phone into a credit card processing machine! Be sure people know to whom to make out personal checks. Don't ask for "cash only". You will miss a lot of sales!

5. Offer a free sign-up for a newsletter, or to enter a contest, or to receive some other benefit. Give people a reason to want to come by your table other than to make a purchase. If at all possible, capture e-mail, phone or other contact information on everyone who attends your event.

We have tons more suggestions to help you maximize sales through in-person "events", so call us if you want help.

Internet Sales Marketing

Much of your marketing will probably involve the internet. The internet affords you many ways to connect with your target audience that are not expensive to do.

The secret to having an effective internet strategy is to engage in these three "C's":

- **CONTENT**
- **COMMERCE**
- **COMMUNITY**

Content—Make sure your website, e-newsletters, and blogs and offer good information and insight at no charge. This content can be excerpted or adapted information from your book. People need to feel there is some valuable information they are getting from you or they won't hang around or come back to your site. So, offer helpful information that makes them want more…and ideally, be willing to pay for it!

Commerce—This simply means you need to have something to sell. Your book, of course, is one thing you can sell, but perhaps you have other resources, or consulting services you can offer for sale through your website. If you don't want to go to the expense and trouble of setting up your own e-commerce software or set up and handle your own product order fulfillment, let us know. HigherLife can offer you e-commerce services that can be linked to your website, so that you can sell your book directly without having to establish complicated and expensive programming to sell products directly on your website. There is no set-up fee for this service.

Community—If you've heard the term Web 2.0, it's referring to how websites today are being used to create dialog and build a sense of belonging and community with the people who come to your site. The phenomenal rise of social media is a reflection of this. To create this sense of community, make sure you ask people to comment on your articles. Ask them to share opinions, take surveys and cast their votes. Do whatever you can to generate a conversation with your readers. It used to be the internet was just a source of information; not anymore. Now, people use the internet as a way to make connections with people. Your internet strategy has to provide ways for people to connect with you, get to know you and feel that you know them.

You want to use the internet to build relationships and create word of mouth "buzz" for your book.

Here are the basic tools you will want to develop for your internet marketing strategy:

- **Website:** Your website is the platform you need to aggressively promote your new brand identity. Websites can be created in all sorts of forms and fashions. Don't spend more than you need to creating an elaborate website that offers more content than is necessary or that you are not willing to keep updated. Make sure you have a presence on the internet.

- **Social Media Marketing:** Once your website is built, you will want to create a sound social media strategy to drive people to your website and make them aware of it. Social media marketing represents the "community" aspect of your internet strategy. It's how you will most easily connect with a wide range of people and draw them to your website where they can order your book. The basics of your social media strategy should include setting up a Facebook account, a Twitter account and developing a blog page linked to your website, or a separate blogsite. Of course, there are hundreds of other social media sites you can set up post to, but these are the basics.

To get started in social media marketing, you should plan to do the following:

1. Regularly post content on your Facebook account including photos and video clips, as well as, plain text. By regularly, I mean daily.

2. Join various user groups and affinity groups available through these social networks.

3. Comment regularly on other people's sites and respond when people comment on your sites.

4. Write a blog at least once a week.

5. Search out what are the highest read blog sites by your target audience. Once you have identified these sites, make comments on their posts and then submit to them excerpts from your book and/or your own posts. If one blogger that's read by tens or hundreds of thousands of people picks up a quote, article or insight from you, then their audience is suddenly introduced to you and many will now want to "follow" you.

All of the above ideas are designed to help you be more "visible" on the internet. Why do you want to be visible? Because if people don't know what you have to offer them to make their life better, they won't be interested in buying your book!

- **Visibility Networking:** Visibility is about being 'seen' in the places your audience hangs out. You need to become a valuable and high profile contributor to the community. This means asking and answering questions; offering advice; and supporting others. These include:
    - Blogs (search on Google for Your Subject + Blog)
    - Add comments (publishing)
    - Write guest articles (publishing)
    - Bookmark good blogs (sharing)
    - Forums (search on Google for Your Subject + Forum)
    - Publishing/sharing/networking
    - Add reviews to relevant books on Amazon (publishing)
    - Add videos to YouTube (publishing)
    - Add photos to Flickr (publishing)

- Add articles to experts sites (Squidoo, Hubpages, eHow, About.com) (publishing)
- Participate in any active communities related to your niche (networking)

I realize this all takes time. Start with what you can manage and expand as necessary. If you don't feel you are getting any results from your efforts, try something else. Just don't give up too early. Like any new relationship, it takes some time for people to get to know you and what you're about.

Specialty Sales Marketing

Specialty sales is a term used to describe sales of your book that you make, usually in bulk quantity, to non-traditional book sales outlets. Specialty sales are harder to come by, but can be quite lucrative. Some book topics lend themselves more readily to specialty sales than others. Some specialty sales outlets are retail venues that are not typically known for selling books. (Depending on the topic, you might sell your book at a farmer's market or a hair salon.) Other specialty sales are made to organizations who purchase your book in bulk quantity. (You may have a friend who owns a large manufacturing plant and wants to give your book out as a gift to all his or her employees or perhaps as a gift to prospects who agree to listen to a sales presentation.

Here are some tips for gaining this kind of sale.

1. Think of businesses, such as insurance companies, health care organizations, attorneys' offices etc, who might be interested in giving your book to their employees, clients or prospects, perhaps as a gift, bonus or part of their continuing education.

2. Think of retailers (other than bookstores) who might be interested in selling your book. Say, for example, you have a book on golf. Could you sell your book at driving ranges and course pro shops?

3. Farmer's markets, fairs, churches are all non-traditional outlets where you could set up a table and sell your book.

4. Could your book be used as a fundraising gift by a school, church or other civic organization? Maybe your school band needs to raise money to buy new uniforms. Could all the students sell your book for $20 and the school gets to keep half that money?

5. Are there conventions such as multi-level-marketing conferences, trade-shows, association sponsored events and other types of conference events where your book could be promoted and/or sold?

6. Are there on-line companies that sell products that appeal to your target audience who might be interested in carrying your book and promoting it through their catalog?

7. Expect to offer fairly high discounts ranging from 50%–70% off the cover price to make a specialty sale. Try to negotiate your sales as "non-returnable".

As you might imagine, the specific topic of your book will lend itself to some specialty sales options more than others.

CHAPTER 12

A Publishing Timeline

With so many steps to the publishing process and so many marketing and sales options to consider, it can be a bit overwhelming to know where to start. You will find it helpful to look at the following simplified twelve-month timeline for publishing and marketing your book. Please understand that getting your book published can take two months or two years and marketing it successfully can last a lifetime. But for the purpose of giving you a helpful framework, I am going to outline what can and should happen throughout the first twelve months of publishing your book.

This timeline assumes that you already have decided to publish a book and have a finished manuscript from which to start. If you're not that far along in the publishing process, I suggest you allow anywhere from six weeks to six months to get your manuscript written or ghostwritten. Understand, the chart below is by no means exhaustive. It's meant merely as a guide to help you get a good overview of the process.

Publishing Timeline

Month	Publishing	Marketing
Month 1	• Publisher Contract Signed • Create a Production Schedule and establish both the author release date and the "pub date" for trade sales • Begin initial content edit	• Create your publishing playbook (see Chapter 1) • Confirm the title & subtitle for the book
Month 2	• Complete initial content edit • Copy editing • Cover copy written • Author Release Date • Trade Release Date	• Create your Strategic Marketing Plan and set sales goals for each of the four main sales channels (See Chapter 10) • Purchase domain names needed • Start building your key contacts database
Month 3	• Have the manuscript copy edited • Get ISBN# and define BISAC information	• Send Advance Review Copies to key trade reviewers • Start collecting endorsements • Set up your website; begin pre-sale strategy

Publishing Timeline		
Month	Publishing	Marketing
Month 4	• Get manuscript interior layout done— Typesetting • Begin final proof-editing	• Start social media strategy • Create special pre-sale offers • Create sales tip sheets for your trade sales team
Month 5	• Make final revisions • Confirm initial print quantity and shipping details • Send to the printers! • Approve press proofs	• Develop your publicity and press kit • Finalize your "free and review" mailing list
Month 6	• Your book is printed and delivered! • Have e-book conversion done	• Upload e-book edition to all sites • Set up your Amazon.com author page
Month 7		• Start blogging excerpts from your book • Begin internet marketing/E-blast campaign
Month 8		• Begin working your daily call/contact sheets • Invite friends to post positive reviews online • Create article excerpts and submit to appropriate media

Publishing Timeline		
Month	Publishing	Marketing
Month 9		• Do "blog tour"
Month 10		• Start posting video excerpts from your book • Announce the general market "trade release" of your book
Month 11		• Host a book launch party • Do an Amazon "Best-seller" campaign on a specified date to drive enough sales to push up your ranking
Month 12		• Start doing as much publicity and author interviews as possible

Remember, this timeline is simply an overview. Every publishing project will have its own unique opportunities and challenges. If you want help with either the publishing or marketing of your book or have questions about what is the best way for you to proceed, please feel free to contact HigherLife. Whether or not you decide to work with us, please know that we can help point you in the right direction.

You don't need to know how to do everything in the publishing or marketing list. This short book has hopefully given you a good baseline of information. At HigherLife, we count it an honor to help you explore the various publishing and marketing options available to you so that you can achieve your publishing dreams. We enjoy helping someone publish a message that will make a difference in our world. So, go make the world a better place and consider making publishing a part of your plan!

IF YOU'RE A FAN OF THIS BOOK, PLEASE TELL OTHERS...

- Write about *Get Your Book Published!* on your blog, Twitter and Facebook page.

- Suggest *Get Your Book Published!* to friends you know who have a book they'd like to publish.

- When you're in a bookstore, ask them if they carry the book. The book is available through all major distributors, so any bookstore that does not have it in stock can easily order it.

- Write a positive review on www.amazon.com.

- Purchase additional copies to give away as gifts. (Just think how many people you know who want to write a book, or who have already written one but want help in marketing it!)

To find out more about how to get your own book published or develop a sound marketing strategy, connect with me at www.ahigherlife.com.

"A BOOK IS THE NEW BROCHURE"
Your story can help grow your business...

 If you run a business and want to more effectively connect with your target audience and get more results from your marketing dollars, I offer proven "Message and Marketing Strategies" that combine the power of "Story" with branding, content marketing and direct-response marketing strategies in a process you won't find anywhere else. For more information go to: www.storymarketingstrategies.com

SPEAKING SCHEDULE...

If you would like to schedule me to speak at your next conference, convention or event, simply e-mail me at info@ahigherlife.com.

MARKET YOUR BOOK...

I've taken the best of what I've learned over the last 30 years of publishing and marketing success and compiled a comprehensive Strategic Book Marketing Plan (SBMP). You could spend countless hours and thousands of dollars to glean what you get from this complete, everything-you-need-to-know strategy. To order go to www.ahigherlife.com.